Hypnotism, Reincarnation And Life After Death

By Ervin Seale

ROOM 206
9 East 40th Street
New York 16, N. Y.

FOREWORD

The main substance of this booklet was first given in a sermon by Dr. Seale at Carnegie Hall. The supply of printed transcripts of that sermon was soon exhausted. It now appears in this form, much enlarged.

When Jesus came into the coast of Caesarea Philippi, he asked his disciples, saying, Whom do men say that I, the Son of man am? And they said, Some say that thou art John the Baptist; some, Elias; and others, Jeremias, or one of the prophets.

He saith unto them, But whom say ye that I am? And Simon Peter answered and said, Thou art the Christ, the Son of the living God. And Jesus answered and said unto him, Blessed art thou, Simon Bar-jona: for flesh and blood hath not revealed it unto thee, but my Father which is in heaven.

Hypnotism, Reincarnation And Life After Death

By Ervin Seale

It may seem strange to some to link hypnotism, reincarnation and life after death together. But Morey Bernstein in his amazing book, "The Search For Bridey Murphy," has awakened a widespread interest in all of these subjects. Hypnotism, especially, has had a revival in the popular mind and great public interest in this fascinating phenomenon of the mind is running at high tide. Hypnotism, as a name for certain phenomena of the mind, is not yet two hundred years old. Before hypnotism was so named, the Mesmerists, as they were called, were producing certain similar phenomena and in many ways more astounding phenomena out of the trance state.

These people were the first mental scientists in modern times. They performed all manner of spectacular cures of disease and demonstrated the higher powers of the subjective mind in man. They showed that

5

there is a level of mind in every man, but dormant in most of us, which lives above time and space, which can actually know and see things and hear things at a distance, irrespective of continents and oceans in between, which can see without eyes, hear without ears and can do all of the other things that our five senses usually do, without the use of the organs of the senses. The ordinary person simply does not dream of the wonder and the magic and the witchery that lie within him.

But the early mesmerists did not know how to explain all of these phenomena any more than modern scientists know how to explain them. They thought they were due to magnetism. And we can understand why they thought so if we recall that this was the pre-electrical age. The Greeks had rubbed the stick of amber with a cat's fur and had discovered static electricity. Our knowledge of electricity had not developed much beyond that point in the eighteenth century when the mesmerists went to work on the human mind.

But there was widespread interest in the phenomenon of magnetism. About this time Benjamin Franklin, here in our own country, flew his kite and discovered something about electricity. Men were fascinated by the uncanny properties of the magnet as revealing some unseen force. So Mesmer and his immediate followers said that the wondrous healings they achieved were produced by animal magnetism, a magnetism which was generated in the human body of the mesmerist and passed to his subject or patient. One of the interesting points about all of this is that while we have, in modern times, set up other explanations of the phenomena of hypnotism and the trance state, we have not yet successfully disproved the theories of the animal magnetists.

Phineas P. Quimby, the discoverer of mental healing in modern times, started as a mesmerist. Through mesmerism he discovered how the human mind works. In his early days he often mesmerized patients for surgery. Though the Eastern world understood these things thousands of years ago, this was the first time in the history of the Western world that men discovered that sensation was not in the flesh but in the mind and if the mind be blocked out by the trance state, the flesh was perfectly anesthetized and no feeling was present;

whereupon, the surgeon could go to work with his knife and the patient would feel no pain.

But with the discovery of anesthesia about 1840, mesmerism fell into disuse. In about 1868 a Scottish physician in England, by the name of James Braid, disputing the claims of the mesmerists that the phenomena were due to animal magnetism, proved that the trance state could be induced by suggestion alone. That is, by speaking to a subject, he could induce the subject to go into a sleep or trance state. He renamed the phenomenon hypnosis after the Greek god of sleep, Hypnos. Hypnosis now had a steady rise in use and popularity and achieved its greatest fame under two famous medical schools in France, one the Salpetriere, presided over by a Dr. Charcot, who laid down the theory that only the hysterical and nervously-diseased people could be hypnotized. The other medical school was the Nancy School, presided over by Drs. Leibault and Bernheim, who took the opposite view from Charcot and showed that hypnosis was not limited to nervous and hysterical people. They did wonderful healing work through hypnosis and proved that thoughts were things and that every thought, by its very nature, tended toward physical expression, manifestation and function.

Emile Coué, a French chemist, followed the examples of these medical men and did the most amazing cures through suggestion and hypnotism, pointing out that the thought of cure alone was sufficient to achieve a cure, that if one would really think of himself as being well, he would by that thinking, set in motion the machinery of cure. Sigmund Freud was a medical man interested in all of the phenomena of the mind and in 1885 went to Paris to study with Charcot and discovered that he could achieve cures by another process, that of allowing the patient to talk and reveal the contents of his own subconscious. So he gave to the world the science of psychoanalysis. After this, hypnosis, as a means of therapy, fell into disuse again and popular interest in it waned.

In the nineteen thirties, there was a short revival of interest in hypnosis when the books of Dr. Alexander Cannon came out and had wide circulation here and abroad. But apart from the stage hypnotists and a limited use of hypnotism among medical men, hypnotism in later years has not had much widespread attention until the emergence of Mr. Bernstein's book. Mr. Bernstein used hypnosis to regress a subject, Ruth Simmons, through the different periods of her life, back to the time of birth and beyond birth into what was presumably another lifetime where she revealed that her name was Bridey Murphy and that she was an Irish girl living in the city of Cork, later moving to Belfast. She named places in Ireland and the names of people who were living contemporaneously with her in Ireland at that time. Altogether, it makes a most fascinating tale of what apparently is a previous lifetime of this Ruth Simmons. It seems to lend great validity to the old Eastern doctrine of reincarnation which holds that human beings live on this earth as in a school, in order to learn certain lessons. When they die, if they have not learned those lessons, they return in other bodies, born of other mothers, to live other lifetimes here on earth. They continue doing this until the lessons are learned and they die and are born no more.

Morey Bernstein frankly hopes that his book will stimulate further research along these lines and that is certainly the broad-gauged attitude we need in regard to these things. So much of the writing on these subjects and especially on the subject of reincarnation is a mere repetition of other men's opinions and beliefs and with little regard for the facts as scientific research proves them to be.

So in order to clarify our understanding of the doctrine of reincarnation somewhat, I want to say next that we are all hypnotized. We are all by our very nature susceptible to the influences, the thoughts, the opinions of other people. From the time we are born into this world we are sensitive, recording mediums upon which the atmospheres, the sights and the sounds of our environment are recorded. Unwittingly and unknowingly our personalities, our temperaments, our dispositions, our very lives are built by influences of which we are mostly unaware. The great law of the mind is this: the subjective self in each of us is amenable to suggestion. Or, as Phineas Quimby puts it, "Man acts as he is acted upon." Quimby refers to the fact that we are all acted upon by atmospheres, influences, concepts and ideas, propaganda and advertising and that we make responses to these influences. If good news comes to the mind, we are elated and we respond in joyfulness and good cheer. If bad news descends upon the mind, it depresses us. So we are the weather vanes of what happens in the world around us, having little inward strength or ability to move on our "own hook," as it were, but always responsively.

The Bible says that we have "all sinned and come short of the glory of God." What does this mean? In our frame of reference it means that we have neglected the great gift and powers of the subjective mind in ourselves which enables each of us to make his life what he wants it to be and we have accepted the limiting beliefs and opinions of men around us and have allowed ourselves to be plunged into inferiority and weakness and poverty and dismay when there is no need of it. In other words we have accepted limitation. Think how a child grows up in an environment which brow-beats it into a sense of inferiority and weakness and all of its life it carries a concept of itself as being inferior to other people and to environment in general. Another child grows up and is scared all of the time. Another person can never seem to make both ends meet but is always in debt and poor in substance. Some people accept the beliefs that they have weak hearts or that certain organs are diseased, that their arthritis is due to the weather, that colds and chronic illnesses are the natural lot of men, never dreaming that much of their discomfort and their pain has been built into them by the ignorance of the racial mind around them and that at any moment they might by a resurgence of the true light within which reveals to them the power of their own mind, throw off this darkness and this spell of limitation. Limitation is simply not true of the real man. We know better because we have seen what is in man and the phenomena of hypnosis has played a very important part in revealing to us the magic and wonders of the subjective man. We know that the subjective of man can receive impressions from the outside world and can act upon them and can turn them into action. We know also that a man experiences exactly what he believes so that, as Solomon says, "As a man thinketh in his heart, so is he."

We know, for example, that if we hypnotize a person in the dead of winter and tell him that he is sitting on the beach, sipping a drink under an umbrella and that the temperature is ninety degrees, his mind, under the influence of this suggestion, will portray for him an entirely different environment from the one he is actually sitting in. His mind will immediately create the environment of the suggestion and project it onto the screen of space and he will be living in it. It is only a short step in our understanding from this revelation to the understanding that we are all living in a world of our own projection.

In a general sense, the physical world is the same for all of us. As we look out of our windows, we here in New York City can see the Empire State Building and the other familiar landmarks. This is the same with all of us. But in a particular sense, each of us sees his own private world with its own private meaning and significance. Each of us is, by the nature of his own subconscious impressions, beliefs and opinions, projecting for himself, his own particular, private world and in it he is living and moving and having his experience. This experience changes constantly as our beliefs and opinions change,

14

as the impressions and ideas which fall upon our recording instruments change; thus our experience changes.

But there is something essential and permanent in our nature beneath all of this changing experience and that is called in the Bible, Christ, or God in us. Thus, in the Bible reading which heads this article, you will discover that Jesus asks Peter the question, "Whom do men say that I am?" And Peter answers, in terms of the beliefs and the opinions of the world mind, "Some say you are Elias, some say you are John the Baptist risen from the dead, some say you are Jeremias or one of the prophets." But Jesus is impatient with all of these answers for they represent only the foolish and unknowing opinions of people who cannot judge except by the surface appearance of things. So He demands, BUT WHOM SAY YE THAT I AM? Finally, Peter answers, THOU ART THE CHRIST, THE SON OF THE LIVING GOD. This is the real truth about any man and about every man — he has God within him. Christ is the Son of God and that Son abides in every human being. It is his divine nature beneath his human nature. This is the great truth of the Bible and of man.

Whenever we see it and understand it, we may throw off the beliefs and opinions and the spells of limitation and exist in our true nature and project a more perfect world for ourselves from more perfect understanding. Until we see this, however, we are forced to play different roles and our experience is a continuous journey between the two sides of our nature. Sometimes we are acting from our Christ center; sometimes we are acting from our human center. Therefore, we are sometimes in misery and sometimes in grandeur and well-being. Again, to quote Dr. Quimby on this subject, "Man is made up of truth and belief." In other words, there is a truth to our nature and it is called Christ or God within us.

When seen and understood, this truth reveals that man has superior powers, that he is the creator and maker of his environment and not the slave of it. That his consciousness projects and makes his world around him. The individual is a creator on the plane of the individual, in harmony with all other individuals and there is, therefore, no conflict, no competition, no antagonists, no opponents and, therefore, nothing to cause resentment, fear or hate or any of the other ugly emotions. But this truth lies deep and dormant in most men and they are, for the most part, ignorant of it. In its place, they accept the beliefs and opinions of the world which are mostly limitation, fear, anger, hate, competition and conflict, resentment and frustration, with the resultant experience of war, disease, and misery.

But the most spell-bound individual never stays wholly in the spell of limitation. There are times when he has glimpses of his Christ-self, and of his real dominion in the world. There are times when he exists in this Christ-self and acts from it. So the common experience for most of us is in traveling back and forth between these two dimensions of ourselves. This transition from one to the other is the Bible's idea of birth and death. Man's common idea of birth and death is far different. The Bible says that the only possible death is to exist under the spell of limitation and inferiority and weakness and that true resurrection from death is to come into the knowledge of one's own Christ powers.

Man's idea is far different. Man believes in two worlds because he has experienced what seems to be two worlds and knows not that there is only one. When a man "dies," as we say in this world, he believes that he is going away from his loved ones and friends and, therefore, by the law of belief, he experiences it in this fashion. Those who are left behind believe also in this separation, that their loved one is leaving them and, therefore, by the law of belief, they experience what they believe. So long as mankind believes in this idea of death, death will be in the world as the common experience of loss and grief, separation and suffering.

But what is the truth about man? Let us reason about it. God is life. Man is one with God. Therefore, man's life is the life of God. This life of God is eternal. That is, it cannot die. God is life in and as the Universal. Man is life in and as the particular. But these are one. There is only one life. It is eternal. That is, it has no beginning and no ending. It is a constant. We have seen that the subjective power in man is creative. There can only be one Creator. If there were two, they would be in conflict. Therefore, there would be no order, no cosmos. By the mathematical necessity of the case, there can be only one Creator. If we find creativity anywhere, we have found that one. We have found creativity in the subjective nature of man, in the quality and the power of his thought and in the projection of his consciousness.

Now listen to this: WE HAVE FOUND THE ONE. This One is the ever-living One, whether considered from the point of view of His universality or his individuality. He is not split up into many individual persons. He is a wholeness manifesting as many individual parts, just as all the land upon this globe is one piece of land, though we see it as individual continents and islands and pieces sticking up above the surface of the ocean. But if we follow them all down, we come to one land mass, a unitary whole. So we are seeing that beneath man's human, changing, suffering nature, there is a permanent and unchanging nature which is stable and abiding and unchanging.

This is the real Man. In this definition, Man is not coming and going anywhere. He is always abiding in the absolute nature of his real self. I am coming now to an explanation of the theory of reincarnation. What we call the individual man is, indeed, an individual entity in universality. It is changeless, permanent and stable. It does not come and go. What does come and go are the beliefs and opinions of men so that every newborn spirit which enters this life in ignorance of its true self is forced by its ignorance to assume the roles which earth life has prepared for it. All around us in this earth atmosphere are the concepts and opinions and atmospheres of men, living and dead. Newborn spirits on the earth plane are forced to take these atmospheres and concepts upon them and to live out these roles until they discover their own Christ and put away the roles which other men have cast for them and discover their own power to project the kind of world they wish.

Think how often in his history man has had to conquer tyranny and to subdue dictators and tyrants and conquerors. Yet, they recur again and again. Brutus killed Caesar and Wellington put down Napoleon but the world tyrants reincarnate, age after age, not because Caesar is a reincarnation of Genghis Khan or because Napoleon is a reincarnation of Caesar or because Hitler or Stalin is a reincarnation of Napoleon (although now, in the afterglow, it seems unworthy to mention Napoleon along with the latter two) but because the idea and concept of tyranny is in the world mind, is in the racial consciousness of man. This is always being reincarnated upon the world stage. Until man puts away his belief in and his fear of tyranny from without, the dictators will always be reincarnated and will scourge the world at periodic ages. Not until man discovers Man will these things cease to be. Then all reincarnation will cease and man will be reborn as Man, as the Man he always was and always will be. Only in his thought did he ever stray from this reality.

This is what Jesus is trying to teach when he is so impatient with Peter who merely babbles about the opinions and beliefs of mankind when he says, "Some say you are this and some say you are that." The doctrine of reincarnation, like so many other doctrines and dogmas of religions of every kind, has become literalized to death and materialized and made gross for childish minds. But it was not always so. Originally it referred to the fact that history repeats itself, that living men are governed by dead men for they merely accept and repeat like parrots, like actors on a stage, the concepts and opinions and beliefs of people long gone from the stage of life.

So what appears like the same individual of another period is actually not the same individuality but is a repetition of the same ideas, beliefs, opinions, temperament and disposition that existed on the stage of life at that former period. The individual entity that manifested at one particular period has gone on and another has taken its place. But they seem like the same person. The only thing that is reincarnated is the role, the personality, the temperament, the human beliefs. But the individual does not reincarnate in the common sense. The real Man is changeless and deathless and birthless. He exists in an absolute condition of being. Therefore, he cannot come and go, he does not travel anywhere.

Where, then, are the dead, so called? Right here. The so-called dead are all about us, separated from us only in our belief. So long as we believe in death, thereby, we shall be separated from our loved ones and our friends. But when we can cast off this spell and understand, as hypnosis so very well shows us, that in our subjective nature we have an existence above time and space, then we shall perceive that those we call separated from us are all about us just as the radio programs and television programs fill this room, though we cannot see them nor hear them without an instrument. But they are all here and probably the only thing that separates us from the so-called dead is frequency, just as frequency separates one television program from another.

Every individual soul in this world or earth experience wears a limiting spirit or influence for a while and then gradually comes to itself. There is no person ever born upon this earth, no matter what his experience, even if he was all of his lifetime a Bowery bum, who has not ascended somewhat in consciousness, though his outward life may not give any evidence of it. That individual entity is going on. I say "going on" because I mean progress but I do not mean going anywhere. I simply mean a rising in consciousness of awareness of the Truth about himself and about life. The limiting role which he played here stays around in the atmosphere of this world and reincarnates in some other spirit.

People draw the easy conclusion that people are born again upon this earth and return to babyhood and go through the process of physical birth. But this is not actually so except in the manner that I have described above. A man never goes backward. He cannot be less tomorrow than he is today. The Bowery bum who goes through years of frustration, fear, suffering, is bound to have some illuminations within, even though he may not be consciously articulate about them. When, as the world says, he "dies," he dies only in our estimation of him. But he lives because he is one with God and death cannot be spoken of in the same breath with God. That man is life, alive with the life of God and, therefore, he cannot die but continues to exist in his absolute nature as an individual entity, part of the universal grandeur that is God and is life. He exists in a dimension or frequency which is hidden from our earth-bound eyes.

I venture one more illustration from the life and science of one of the most amazing but one of the least known of the men of our modern times, Phineas P. Quimby, who as I have mentioned, began his career as a mesmerist. Surgeons often called upon Dr. Quimby to mesmerize a patient for surgery. On one occasion he had mesmerized a woman who had a needle embedded in her arm. Quimby put her in the trance and the surgeon after determining that her flesh was in anesthesia, began the surgical removal of the needle, while Quimby watched. Presently, the woman began to speak out of her trance state and, addressing herself to Quimby, said, "Does it not hurt you?" He answered, "No." And she said, "I should think it would."

This revealed to Quimby — and it was probably the first time it came to the attention of any mesmerist, though it is lost to the literature of the field because Quimby is unknown and his fragmentary writings are largely unpublished — that in the hypnotic trance or the subjective state, the subject associates himself almost entirely with the personality and the conscious intelligence of the operator. In the literature of hypnosis it is called the state of rapport, which means that every thought the operator thinks, is registered in the subject and he responds accordingly. It has even been shown that the rhythm of the breath of the operator and subject is in harmony.

In the phenomena of hypnosis it has often been shown that the subject registers the operator's beliefs and opinions very faithfully. Two different hypnotists will often get two different results with the same subject. In the case of the woman here mentioned, her conscious intelligence was in abeyance and Quimby's was substituted for it. So, in her subjective state, she thought of herself as Quimby, looking upon her own body. Therefore, she spoke in the way just related. This was one of those early experiments which laid the basis for a true science of the mind and which has been the precious property of metaphysicians ever since. It showed that the subject has no conscious awareness, that his personality and conscious mind have been displaced by the operator's. Hence, all he knows of the objective world is what the operator knows, or at least, all that he will respond to. He strives mightily to give the operator what he wants and the operator may not know exactly what he wants but his beliefs and opinions about life in general will adduce a corresponding response from his subject in the trance.

Therefore, we may consider the validity of the suggestion that Bridey Murphy could be in Morey Bernstein. It is a view that has to be considered. It is a field wherein much future research must be done. It is a subject which all future research will have to consider. As Bernstein himself says, "We have so little to lose and so much to gain by continuing to trace the reach of the mind."

I repeat that there are many personality roles in the world and that these persist from age to age in the racial consciousness. It is these which reincarnate year after year and age after age. You and I, as temporarily earth-bound beings, have our choice of many roles. If we repeat the past and play the ready-made roles of ignorance and frustration and fear and conflict, then this role has found reincarnation in and through us. But we ourselves are just what we have always been and what we always shall be, an absolute, birthless, deathless, regnant, sovereign, spiritual being, having a life and an existence above and outside of time and space and all frustration, suffering and decay. "Because He lives, we shall live also." The mystery of life, as Paul suggests, is this, that "we shall not all die but we shall all be changed." We shall have to change to a concept of our true and sovereign self. That is why the Great Authority in life demands an answer to one significant and pertinent question. "Whom do ye say that I am?" And this Great Authority is within every individual and weeps when the individual cannot believe in Him and is constantly urging you as a personality to throw off your inferiority and your weakness, your misery and your unhappiness and accept your true God-self and die and be born to human opinion no more.

All of us as individuals live in a vast cosmic continuum of universal consciousness which I have called the World Mind, not to be confused with what the New Testament refers to as the world, meaning the racial mind. This World Mind is Universal Wisdom and Universal Love and Universal Power. What we call our Private Minds are only Participating Centers in this World Mind. Actually, there is no such thing as a Private Mind. Our Private Minds are the Universal Mind individualized. Now, whenever you individualize or particularize anything you shut out a great deal more than you include. Thus, Individual Mind by its very nature, is limited, isolated and operates within boundaries. But these boundaries are mental only and they are flexible. As in a chemical laboratory a thin membrane can be placed between two different solutions in a glass container and by the process known as osmosis the solutions will mix or exchange through the membrane; so in times of prayer, sleep, inspiration or enchantment an analogous process takes place between our Individual Mind and the Universal Mind. Then we have in the Individual Mind more Wisdom and more Power, consequently less limitation and restriction. The more fascinated and absorbed the Individual or Personal Mind becomes with phenomena, the more it falls out of touch with the World Mind or the thicker and more impenetrable the membrane becomes. Then the Personal Mind which we also call the Conscious Mind is said to fall asleep in matter and its sensations. The Bible calls this condition death and the grave. "The grave cannot praise thee. . . . There is neither knowledge nor wisdom in the grave." The Psalmist asks, "Shall thy loving kindness be declared in

29

the grave? . . . shall thy wonders be known in the dark? and thy righteousness in the land of forgetfulness? (88). Of course not. The Personal Mind commonly knows little or nothing about the World Mind and hence cannot praise it. Yet this is what it must do eventually and it does come around to it at last in all men. And this coming around to conscious union with the World Mind is called in the Bible the resurrection from the dead. Now this may be a strange concept to you if you have been schooled to believe in a literal death and a literal resurrection. But by the facts of the case this must be so. God is Life. You are alive. God cannot die. Therefore you cannot die. What is this thing called death then if it is not a lapse from our true nature, a waywardness that is for a time only, a failure to participate fully in the Largeness of Being, a hesitancy to accept the Infinitude of that which seems so finite.

Man has Another Self than that which he ordinarily experiences and it is in this Other Self that his salvation lies. The phenomena of hypnosis, spiritualism and trance show the glorious powers of this Other Self. Its extra-sensory perceptions, its freedom of time and space, its dominance over pain and suffering of all kinds, its ability to participate in otherwise hidden knowledge and "to fetch wisdom from afar," all these and many more reveal something in man that far transcends his intellect and personality and causes him to wonder, to worship and to praise. The Subjective Self in man is really the World Mind participating in Personal Consciousness. It is this that builds and maintains the body and without interference from the Conscious Mind will maintain it perfectly. It is this Other Self participating in human consciousness that saves, redeems and anchors a person in the heavenly kingdom. That is why I believe in the Christian doctrine of the Vicarious Atonement. We are saved already. This Other Self has redeemed us. Orthodox Christianity teaches that if you believe in Jesus Christ and accept Jesus as your personal Lord and Saviour, you are saved, redeemed and accepted as a candidate for heavenly bliss. I say, If you believe in your Other Self or in the participating activity of the World Mind — call it Soul or Oversoul if you prefer; I do not propose to limit it by a term — then you are saved from your tormentors in this world and in the next, you are freed of pain, sorrow, limitation of all sorts and descriptions and what is more: nothing shall be impossible unto you.

It is because you live in this World Mind and it lives in you that you have often met a person and felt that you had known him before. Perhaps you had no other explanation than that you and he had been together in a previous incarnation. That, indeed, is one way of explaining it. Also, you have come to a certain place for the first time in this life and felt strongly that you had been there before. All seemed familiar to you. But remember that in your Higher Dimension of World Mind you have been everywhere and seen everything. Nothing is hidden. All is known. The mist of forgetfulness has cleared more in certain areas of consciousness than in others and these seem more familiar as though known of old. In terms of the Universal Presence, there is no Here and There, no Now and Then. "These be the whims of mortal mind" and describe the experience as it looks from the sensation side. Full understanding requires a description from the point of view of the other side.

We shall never be more immortal than we are at this moment. The Subconscious (part of the World Mind) is a recording medium. All of our realizations are recorded there. A wealth of evidence, checked and rechecked shows that the Subjective Entity does not die with the body. It continues with its realizations. It continues as before. Death is in those who believe it to be "gone" and not in itself. Earth means much more than just this particular planet. Earth as a Biblical and occult terms means manifestation. Heaven means the unmanifested realms of consciousness. Our only journey is between these two recurrently. By the law of the mind that as a man thinketh in his heart so is he, all of our realizations are projected into form and experience or "earth." But that "earth" may be far different from anything known in the "earth" previously. "Behold, I make new heavens and new earths." Our life is now eternal. Our individuality is imperishable. Reincarnation is a description of that Eternal Life from the point of view of time and space. To think of ourselves only in these terms is a grievous bondage. To meditate frequently upon the Higher Identity and its absence of movement, its freedom from struggle and from all change and turbulence is to thin down the membrane of fixed opinion that separates our consciousness from Total Good. It is to enter into that Great Good now without the need for struggle and trial-and-error-experience. "Lift up your eyes and look on the fields; for they are white already to harvest."

NOTES

WRITINGS OF ERVIN SEALE

Ten Words That Will Change Your Life 2.50
Learn to Live—The Meaning of the Parables........... 2.75
The Greater Prayer (Interpretation of the Lord's
Prayer 1.75
Reformers and Informers .... .25
Seven Eyes and a Stone 25
The Prayer That Changes Things .... .25
How to Use your Senses .... .25
Delivery From Fear .... .25
Accidents and Acts of God (The Cause of Accidents) .25
Little Essays on Truth No. 1 . ... .25
Little Essays on Truth No. 2 .. .. .25
Little Essays on Truth No. 3 .... .25
The Five Finger Exercise (A Prayer Formula) .... .15
Bless It - A Card .... .05
The Silence (A Guide to Meditation) .... .05
Self Treatment (A Guide to Meditation) .... .05
Imagineering .... .15
Overcoming Resentment .... .25
Better Health Through Mind .... .15
Your Mind Is a Magnet 15
My Country .... .25
From Death to Life (On Lent) .... .10
The Shepherd Psalm (Interpretation Psalm 23) .... .05
The Church of the Truth in New York 10
Back Copies of The Builder - per copy .. .. .35
THE BUILDER, Published Monthly, - per year 3.50
(One of Dr. Seale's Sunday Addresses each month)

QUIMBY LITERATURE

The Philosophy of P. P. Quimby by Annetta Dresser 2.00
The True History of Mental Science
by Julius Dresser   ..   .. .50

order from

THE BUILDER PRESS

9 East 40th Street, Room 206

New York 16, New York

CPSIA information can be obtained
at www.ICGtesting.com
Printed in the USA
LVHW080225171220
674407LV00014B/841

9 781162 921761